CAMPFIRE SONGS
FOR UKULELE

2	AMIE
6	BLOWIN' IN THE WIND
8	BROWN EYED GIRL
14	THE CAMPFIRE SONG SONG
11	DON'T WORRY, BE HAPPY
23	DRIFT AWAY
16	EDELWEISS
18	FOLSOM PRISON BLUES
20	THE GAMBLER
29	GOD BLESS THE U.S.A.
26	HALLELUJAH
32	HELLO MUDDUH, HELLO FADDUH! (A LETTER FROM CAMP)
38	THE HOUSE OF THE RISING SUN
40	I WALK THE LINE
42	I'D LIKE TO TEACH THE WORLD TO SING
44	LEAN ON ME
35	LEAVING ON A JET PLANE
47	LET IT BE
57	THE LION SLEEPS TONIGHT
50	MOUNTAIN DEW
52	ON TOP OF SPAGHETTI
54	PEACEFUL EASY FEELING
60	PUFF THE MAGIC DRAGON
66	SUNDOWN
63	TAKE ME HOME, COUNTRY ROADS
68	THIS LAND IS YOUR LAND
70	TIE ME KANGAROO DOWN SPORT
72	THE UNICORN
75	WAGON WHEEL
78	YOU ARE MY SUNSHINE

ISBN 978-1-4803-9420-9

HAL•LEONARD®

T0057855

Amie

Words and Music by Craig Fuller

First note

Verse
Moderately, in 2

1. I can see why you think you be-long ___ to me; ___
2., 4. *See additional lyrics*
3. *Instrumental*

I nev-er tried to make ___ you think or let ___

___ you see one ___ thing for your-self. ___

But now you're off with some-one else, ___ and I'm ___ a - lone. ___

___ You see, I thought that I ___ might _

© 1975 (Renewed) UNICHAPPELL MUSIC INC. and MCKENZIE MUSIC
All Rights Administered by UNICHAPPELL MUSIC INC.
All Rights Reserved   Used by Permission

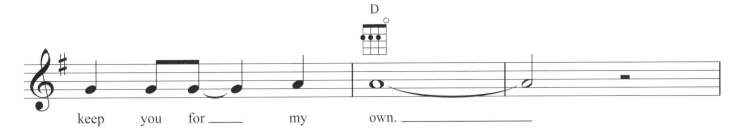

keep you for ____ my own. _____

Chorus

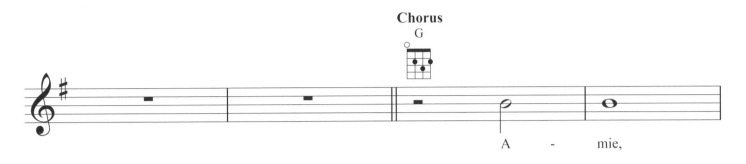

A - mie,

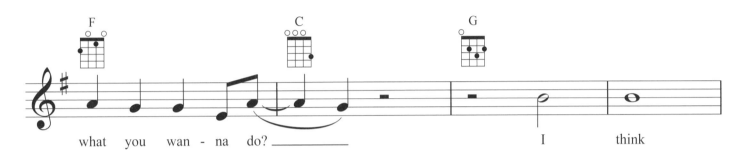

what you wan - na do? _____ I think

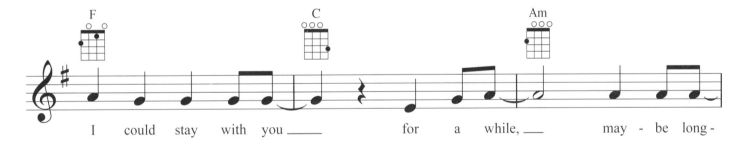

I could stay with you ____ for a while, ___ may - be long-

To Coda ⊕ **Interlude**

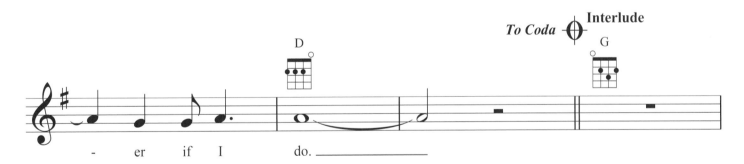

- er if I do. _____

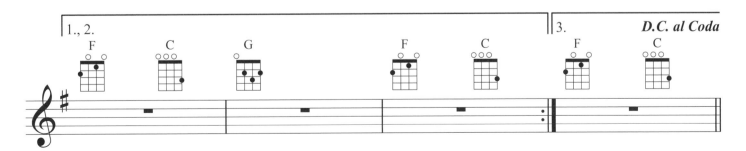

Coda

Chorus

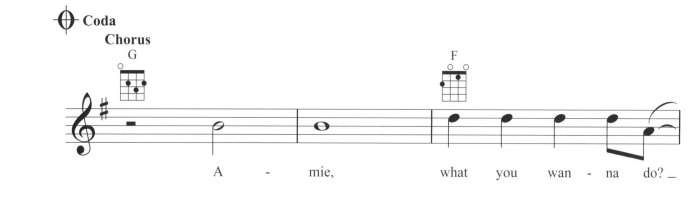

A - mie, what you wan - na do? __

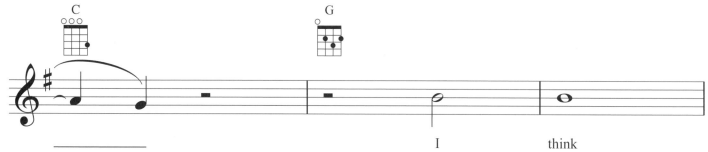

_____ I think

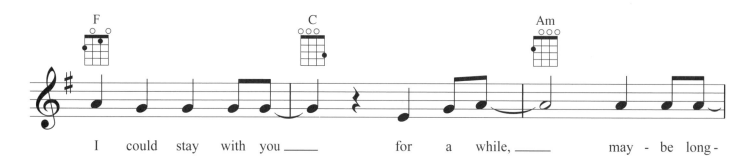

I could stay with you _____ for a while, _____ may - be long-

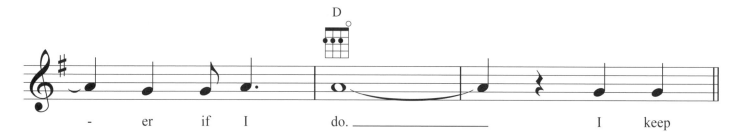

- er if I do. _____ I keep

Outro

fall - in' in and out ___ of love _____ with you, __

_____ fall - in' in and out ___ of love __

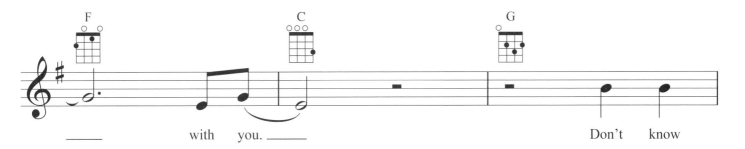

with you. _____ Don't know

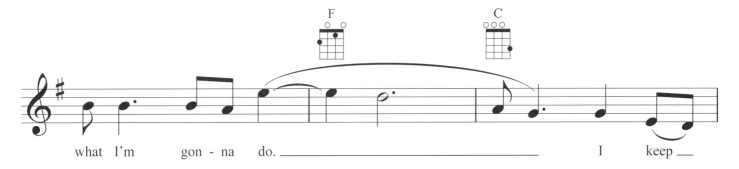

what I'm gon - na do. _____ I keep _____

fall - in' in and out _____ of love _____

with you. _____

_____

Additional Lyrics

2. Don't you think the time is right for us to find
All the things we thought weren't proper?
Could be right in time, and can you see
Which way we should turn together or alone?
I can never see what's right or what is wrong.
Would it take too long to see?

4. Now it's come to what you want; you've had your way.
And all the things you thought before
Just faded into gray, and can you see
That I don't know if it's you or if it's me?
If it's one of us, I'm sure we both will see.
Won't ya look at me and tell me...

Blowin' in the Wind

Words and Music by Bob Dylan

Verse
Moderately fast

1. How man-y roads _____ must a man _____ walk _ down _
2., 3. *See additional lyrics*

_____ be - fore _____ you call _____ him a man? _____

How man - y seas _____ must a white _____ dove _ sail _

_____ be - fore _____ she sleeps in the sand? _____

Yes, and how _____ man - y times _____ must the can -

Copyright © 1962 Warner Bros. Inc.
Copyright Renewed 1990 Special Rider Music
International Copyright Secured   All Rights Reserved
Reprinted by Permission of Music Sales Corporation

non - balls ___ fly ___ be - fore ___ they are for -

- ev - er banned? ___ The an -

Chorus

- swer, my friend, ___ is blow - in' in ___ the wind. ___

___ The an - swer is blow - in' in ___ the wind. ___

|1., 2. | 3.

Additional Lyrics

2. How many years can a mountain exist
    Before it is washed to the sea?
    How many years can some people exist
    Before they're allowed to be free?
    Yes, and how many times can a man turn his head
    And pretend that he just doesn't see?

3. How many times must a man look up
    Before he can see the sky?
    How many ears must one man have
    Before he can hear people cry?
    Yes, and how many deaths will it take till he knows
    That too many people have died?

Brown Eyed Girl

Words and Music by Van Morrison

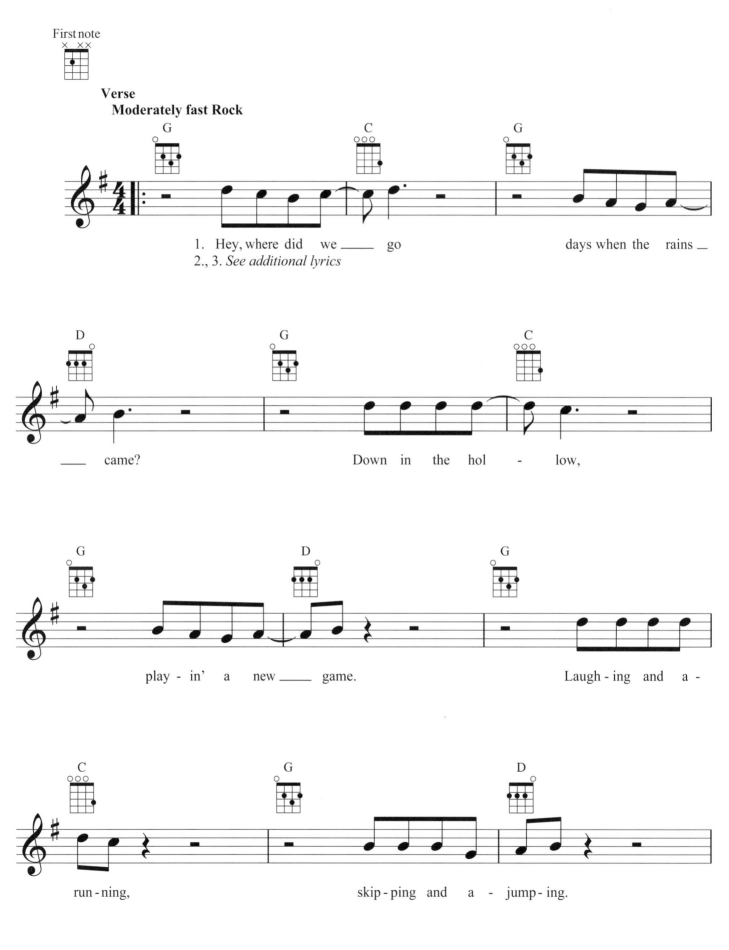

Copyright © 1967 UNIVERSAL MUSIC PUBLISHING INTERNATIONAL LTD.
Copyright Renewed
All Rights for the U.S. and Canada Controlled and Administered by UNIVERSAL - SONGS OF POLYGRAM INTERNATIONAL, INC.
All Rights Reserved   Used by Permission

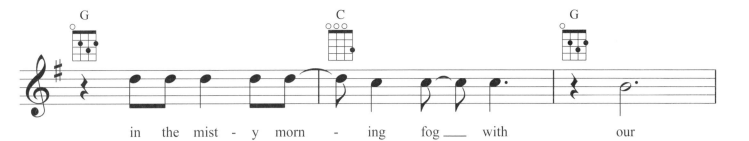

in the mist - y morn - ing fog ___ with our

hearts a - thump - in', and you, _____ my brown eyed girl. ___

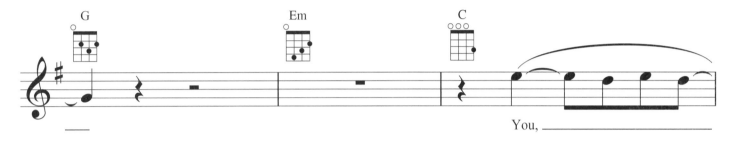

You, _____

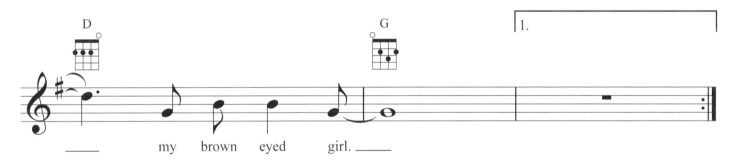

1.

___ my brown eyed girl. ___

2., 3.

Do you re - mem - ber when ___ we used to sing: ___

Chorus

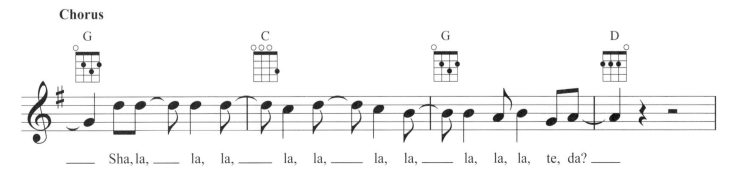

___ Sha, la, ___ la, la, ___ la, la, ___ la, la, ___ la, la, la, te, da? ___

Additional Lyrics

2. Whatever happened
   To Tuesday and so slow?
   Going down the old mine
   With a transistor radio.
   Standing in the sunlight laughing,
   Hiding behind a rainbow's wall,
   Slipping and sliding
   All along the waterfall with you,
   My brown eyed girl.
   You, my brown eyed girl.

3. So hard to find my way
   Now that I'm all on my own.
   I saw you just the other day;
   My, how you have grown.
   Cast my mem'ry back there, Lord.
   Sometimes I'm overcome thinking 'bout it.
   Laughing and a-running, hey, hey,
   Behind the stadium with you,
   My brown eyed girl.
   You, my brown eyed girl.

Don't Worry, Be Happy

Words and Music by Bobby McFerrin

Copyright © 1988 by Probnoblem Music
All Rights in the United States and Canada Administered by Universal Music - Careers
International Copyright Secured   All Rights Reserved

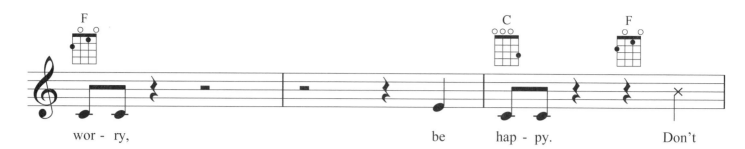

wor - ry, be hap - py. Don't

Chorus

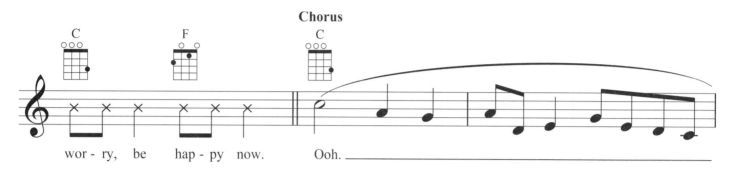

wor - ry, be hap - py now. Ooh. _____

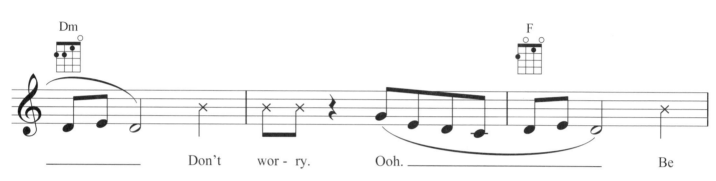

_____ Don't wor - ry. Ooh. _____ Be

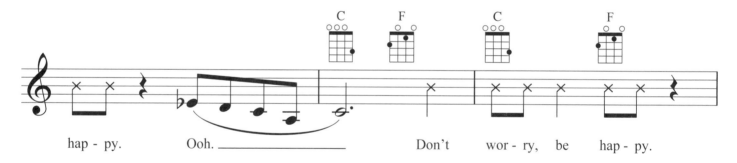

hap - py. Ooh. _____ Don't wor - ry, be hap - py.

Ooh. _____ Don't

To Coda ⊕

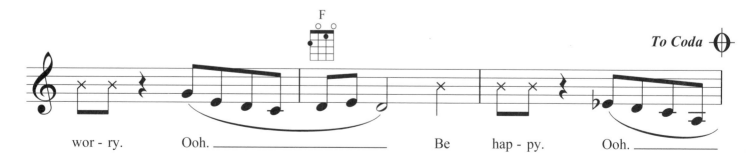

wor - ry. Ooh. _____ Be hap - py. Ooh. _____

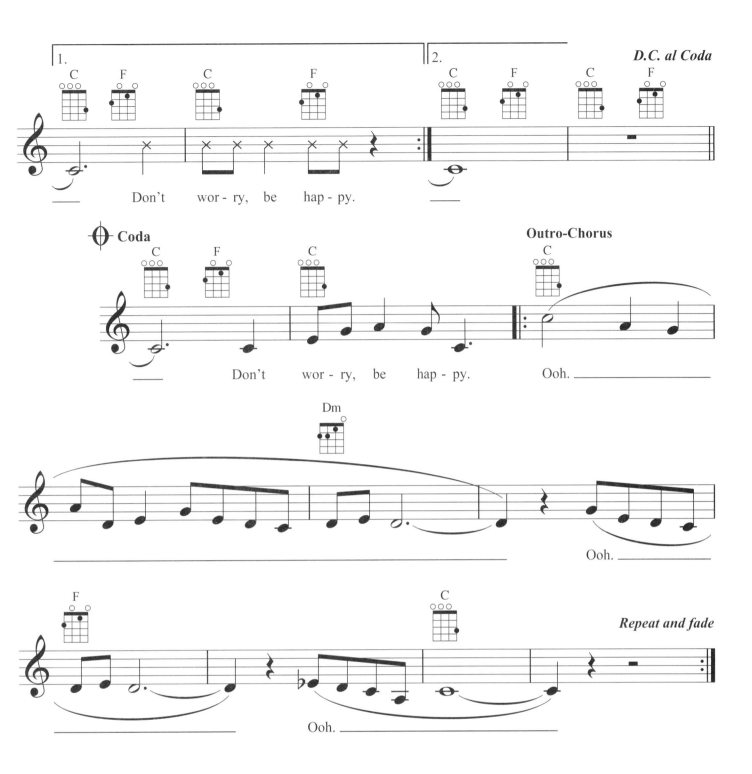

Don't wor - ry, be hap - py.

Coda

Outro-Chorus

Don't wor - ry, be hap - py. Ooh. _____

Ooh. _____

Ooh. _____ Ooh. _____

Additional Lyrics

2. Ain't got no place to lay your head.
   Somebody came and took your bed.
   Don't worry, be happy.
   The landlord say your rent is late,
   He may have to litigate.
   Don't worry, be happy.
   (Spoken:) Look at me— I'm happy.

3. Ain't got no cash, ain't got no style.
   Ain't got no gal to make you smile.
   Don't worry, be happy.
   'Cause when you worry your face will frown,
   And that will bring ev'rybody down.
   Don't worry, be happy.
   Don't worry, be happy now.

The Campfire Song Song

from SPONGEBOB SQUAREPANTS

Words and Music by Carl Williams, Dan Povenmire, Jay Lender, Michael Culross and Michael Walker

Let chord ring.

Copyright © 2002 Music by Nickelodeon Inc.
All Rights Administered by Sony/ATV Music Publishing LLC, 424 Church Street, Suite 1200, Nashville, TN 37219
International Copyright Secured   All Rights Reserved

Chorus (faster each time)

C-A-M-P-F-I-R-E S-O-N-G song.

C-A-M-P-F-I-R-E S-O-N-G song. And if

you don't think that we can sing it fast - er, then you're

wrong. But it - 'll help if you just sing a - long. _____

wrong. It - 'll help, _____ it - 'll

help _____ if you just sing a - long.

Edelweiss

from THE SOUND OF MUSIC
Lyrics by Oscar Hammerstein II
Music by Richard Rodgers

Copyright © 1959 by Richard Rodgers and Oscar Hammerstein II
Copyright Renewed
Williamson Music, a Division of Rodgers & Hammerstein: an Imagem Company, owner of publication and allied rights throughout the world
International Copyright Secured   All Rights Reserved

Bridge

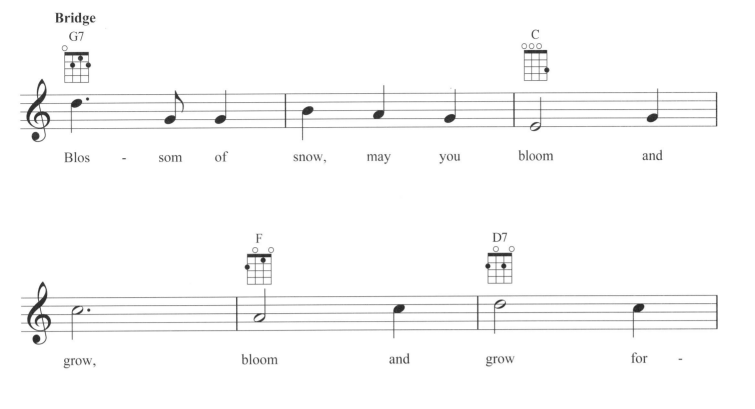

Blos - som of snow, may you bloom and

grow, bloom and grow for -

Chorus

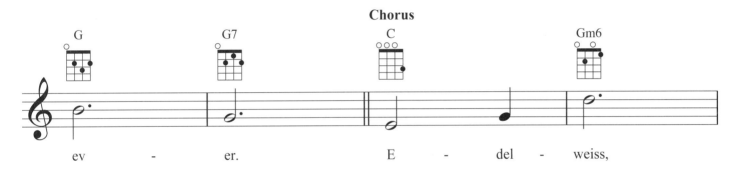

ev - er. E - del - weiss,

e - del - weiss, bless my

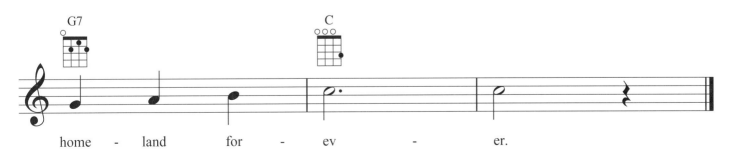

home - land for - ev - er.

Folsom Prison Blues

Words and Music by John R. Cash

First note

Verse
Moderately, in 2

1. I hear the train a - com - in', it's
(2.–4.) *See additional lyrics*

roll - in' 'round the bend, ____ and I ain't seen the sun-

- shine since I don't ___ know when. I'm

stuck in Fol - som Pris - on and time keeps

© 1956 (Renewed 1984) HOUSE OF CASH, INC. (BMI)/Administered by BUG MUSIC INC., A BMG CHRYSALIS COMPANY
All Rights for the World outside the U.S. Administered by UNICHAPPELL MUSIC, INC.
All Rights Reserved   Used by Permission

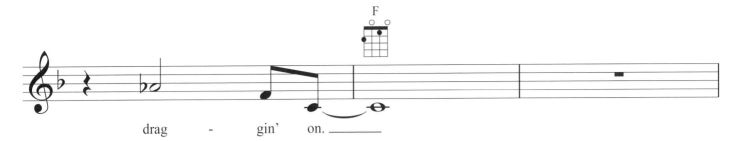

drag - gin' on. _____

But that train keeps a roll -

- in' on down to San _____ An -

tone.

1.–3.

4.

2. When
3. I
4. Well, if they

Additional Lyrics

2. When I was just a baby, my mama told me, "Son,
   Always be a good boy; don't ever play with guns."
   But I shot a man in Reno, just to watch him die.
   When I hear that whistle blowin', I hang my head and cry.

3. I bet there's rich folks eatin' in a fancy dining car.
   They're prob'ly drinkin' coffee and smokin' big cigars.
   Well, I know I had it comin', I know I can't be free.
   But those people keep a-movin' and that's what tortures me.

4. Well, if they freed me from this prison, if that railroad train was mine,
   I bet I'd move it on a little farther down the line.
   Far from Folsom Prison, that's where I want to stay,
   And I'd let that lonesome whistle blow my blues away.

The Gambler

Words and Music by Don Schlitz

Copyright © 1977 Sony/ATV Music Publishing LLC
Copyright Renewed
All Rights Administered by Sony/ATV Music Publishing LLC, 424 Church Street, Suite 1200, Nashville, TN 37219
International Copyright Secured   All Rights Reserved

- ble.   There'll   be   time   e - nough ___   for   count -

- in'   when   the   deal - in's

done.   4. Now,   done.

Additional Lyrics

2. He said, "Son, I've made my life out of readin' people's faces,
   And knowin' what their cards were by the way they held their eyes.
   So if you don't mind me sayin', I can see you're out of aces.
   For a taste of your whiskey, I'll give you some advice."

3. So, I handed him my bottle and he drank down my last swallow.
   Then he bummed a cigarette and asked me for a light.
   And the night got deathly quiet, and his face lost all expression,
   Said, "If you're gonna play the game, boy, you gotta learn to play it right."

4. Now, ev'ry gambler knows the secret to survivin'
   Is knowing what to throw away and knowin' what to keep.
   'Cause ev'ry hand's a winner and ev'ry hand's a loser,
   And the best you can hope for is to die in your sleep.

5. So, when he'd finished speakin', he turned back toward the window,
   Crushed out his cigarette and faded off to sleep.
   Then somewhere in the darkness, the gambler, he broke even,
   But in his final words I found an ace that I could keep.

Drift Away

Words and Music by Mentor Williams

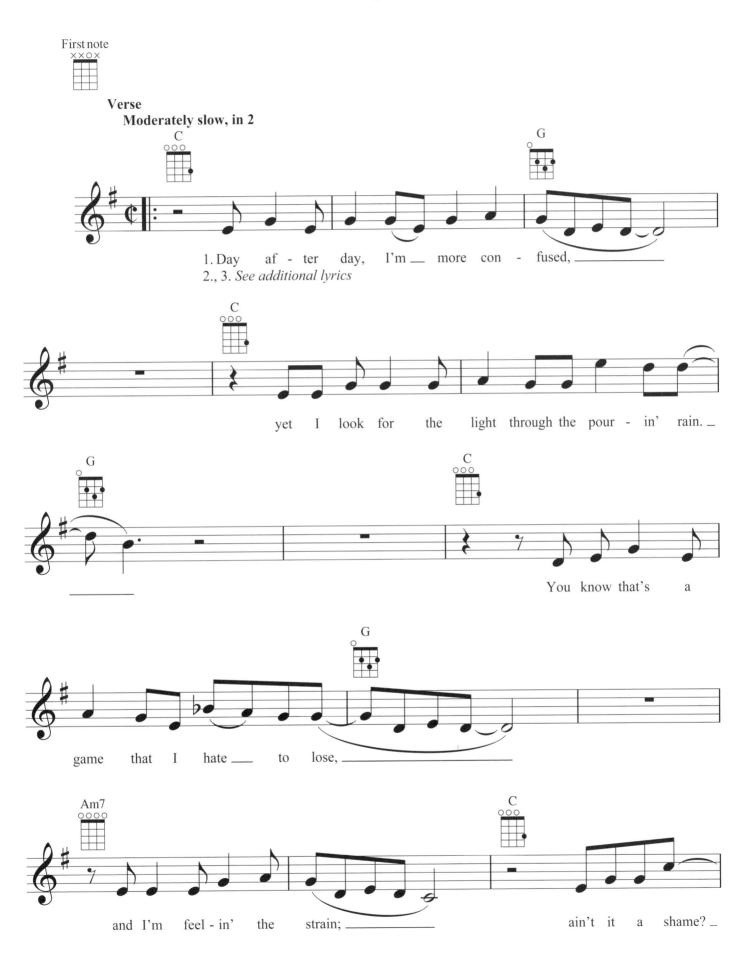

Copyright © 1972 ALMO MUSIC CORP.
Copyright Renewed
All Rights Reserved   Used by Permission

Chorus

G

— Oh, give me the beat, __ boys, and free my soul. __ I

D   C

wan - na get lost in your rock and roll __ and drift a - way. __

G

Oh, give me the beat, __ boys, and free my soul. __ I

D   C

wan - na get lost in your rock and roll __ and drift a - way. __

To Coda ⊕

(Instrumental)

G   D7sus4   G

24

Additional Lyrics

2. Beginnin' to think that I'm wastin' time.
   I don't understand the things I do.
   The world outside looks so unkind,
   And I'm countin' on you to carry me through.

3. Thanks for the joy that you've given me.
   I want you to know I believe in your song
   And rhythm and rhyme and harmony.
   You help me along, makin' me strong.

Hallelujah

Words and Music by Leonard Cohen

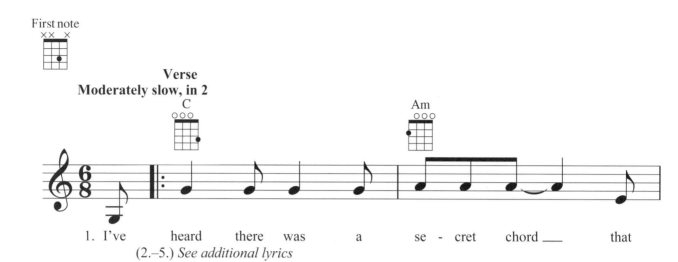

Verse
Moderately slow, in 2

1. I've heard there was a se - cret chord ___ that
(2.–5.) *See additional lyrics*

Da - vid played ___ and it pleased the Lord, ___ but you don't ___ real - ly

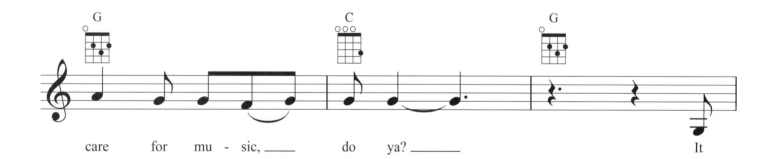

care for mu - sic, ___ do ya? _____ It

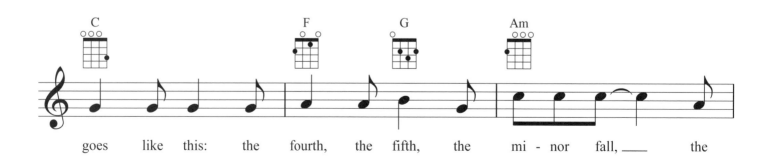

goes like this: the fourth, the fifth, the mi - nor fall, ___ the

Copyright © 1985 Sony/ATV Music Publishing LLC
All Rights Administered by Sony/ATV Music Publishing LLC, 424 Church Street, Suite 1200, Nashville, TN 37219
International Copyright Secured   All Rights Reserved

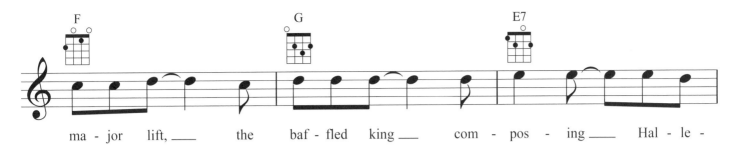

ma - jor lift, ___ the baf - fled king ___ com - pos - ing ___ Hal - le -

Chorus

lu - jah. _____ Hal - le - lu - jah, _____ hal - le -

lu - jah, _____ hal - le - lu - jah, _____ hal - le -

1.–4.

lu - jah. 2. Your

Outro-Chorus

5.

lu - jah. Hal - le - lu - jah. _____ Hal - le -

lu - jah. _____ Hal - le - lu - jah. _____ Hal - le -

lu - jah. _____

Additional Lyrics

2. Your faith was strong but you needed proof.
   You saw her bathing on the roof.
   Her beauty and the moonlight overthrew ya.
   She tied you to a kitchen chair.
   She broke your throne, she cut your hair.
   And from your lips she drew the Hallelujah.

3. Maybe I have been here before.
   I know this room, I've walked this floor.
   I used to live alone before I knew ya.
   I've seen your flag on the marble arch.
   Love is not a vict'ry march.
   It's a cold and it's a broken Hallelujah.

4. There was a time you let me know
   What's real and going on below.
   But now you never show it to me, do ya?
   And remember when I moved in you.
   The holy dove was movin', too,
   And every breath we drew was Hallelujah.

5. Maybe there's a God above,
   And all I ever learned from love
   Was how to shoot at someone who outdrew ya.
   And it's not a cry you can hear at night.
   It's not somebody who's seen the light.
   It's a cold and it's a broken Hallelujah.

God Bless the U.S.A.

Words and Music by Lee Greenwood

Copyright © 1984 SONGS OF UNIVERSAL, INC. and UNIVERSAL - SONGS OF POLYGRAM INTERNATIONAL, INC.
All Rights Controlled and Administered by SONGS OF UNIVERSAL, INC.
All Rights Reserved   Used by Permission

pride in ev-'ry A-mer-i-can heart, and it's time to stand and say _____ that I'm

Coda   **Outro-Chorus**

A. _____   And I'm proud to be an A-mer-i-can ___ where at

least I know I'm free. And I won't for-get the men who died, ___ who

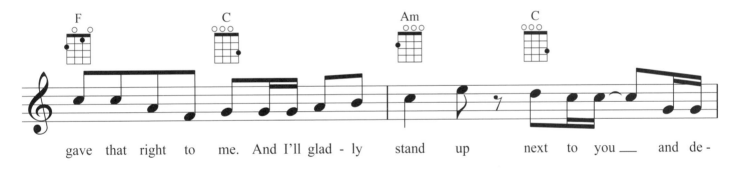

gave that right to me. And I'll glad-ly stand up next to you ___ and de-

fend her still to-day, 'cause there ain't no doubt I love this land. ___

_____ God bless the U. S. A.

Hello Mudduh, Hello Fadduh!
(A Letter from Camp)
Words by Allan Sherman
Music by Lou Busch

© 1963 (Renewed) WB MUSIC CORP. and BURNING BUSH MUSIC
All Rights Reserved   Used by Permission

i - vy.   You re - mem - ber   Leo - nard   Skin - ner?   He got
lar - ia.   You re - mem - ber   Jef - frey   Har - dy?   They're a -

pto - maine poi - s'ning last night af - ter   din - ner.   2. All the
bout to or - gan - ize a search - ing   par - ty.

Bridge

Take   me   home,   oh, Mud - duh, Fad - duh, take   me
Take   me   home,   I prom - ise I will   not   make

home,   I hate Gra - na - da. Don't   leave   me   out   in   the for - est
noise,   or mess the house with   oth - er   boys.   Oh, please don't make me

1.

where   I   might   get   eat - en   by   a   bear.

2.

stay;   I've been   here   one   whole   day!   3. Dear - est

Leaving on a Jet Plane

Words and Music by John Denver

Copyright © 1967; Renewed 1995 BMG Ruby Songs and BMG Rights Management (Ireland), Ltd.
All Rights for BMG Ruby Songs Administered by BMG Rights Management (US) LLC
International Copyright Secured   All Rights Reserved

Chorus

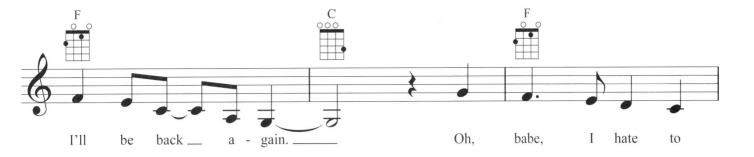

I'll be back __ a - gain. _____ Oh, babe, I hate to

1., 2.

3.

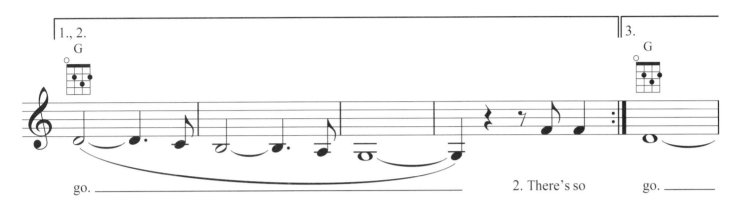

go. _____ 2. There's so go. _____

Outro

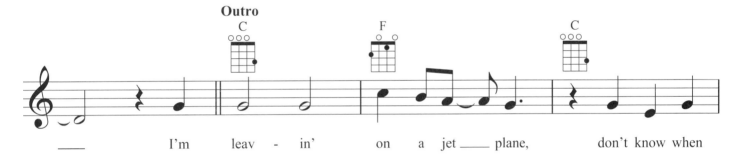

__ I'm leav - in' on a jet __ plane, don't know when

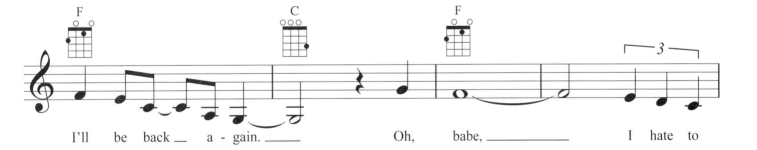

I'll be back __ a - gain. _____ Oh, babe, _____ I hate to

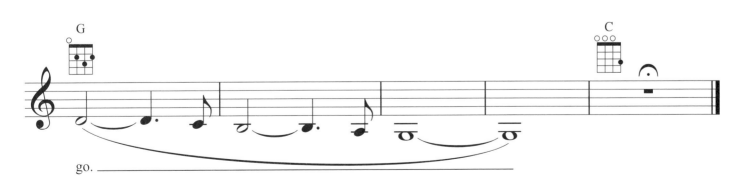

go. _____

The House of the Rising Sun

Words and Music by Alan Price

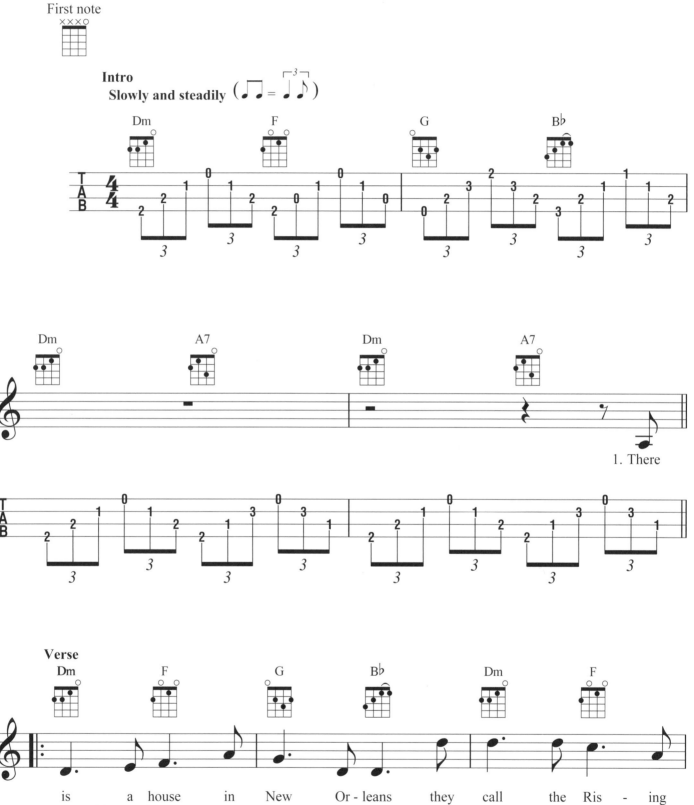

is   a   house   in   New   Or - leans   they   call   the   Ris - ing

(2.–6.) *See additional lyrics*

© 1964 (Renewed 1992) KEITH PROWSE MUSIC PUBLISHING CO., LTD.
All Rights Reserved   International Copyright Secured   Used by Permission

Additional Lyrics

2. My mother was a tailor, sewed my new blue jeans.
   My father was a gamblin' man down in New Orleans.

3. Now, the only thing a gambler needs is a suitcase and a trunk.
   And the only time he'll be satisfied is when he's on a drunk.

4. Oh! mother, tell your children not to do what I have done:
   Spend your lives in sin and misery in the House of the Rising Sun.

5. Well, I've got one foot on the platform, the other foot on the train.
   I'm going back to New Orleans to wear that ball and chain.

6. Well, there is a house in New Orleans they call the Rising Sun.
   And it's been the ruin of many a poor boy, and God, I know I'm one.

I Walk the Line

Words and Music by John R. Cash

© 1956 (Renewed 1984) HOUSE OF CASH, INC./Administered by BUG MUSIC, INC., A BMG CHRYSALIS COMPANY
All Rights outside the U.S. Controlled by UNICHAPPELL MUSIC INC.
All Rights Reserved   Used by Permission

Additional Lyrics

3. As sure as night is dark and day is light,
   I keep you on my mind both day and night.
   And happiness I've known proves that it's right.
   Because you're mine, I walk the line.

4. You've got a way to keep me on your side.
   You give me a cause for love that I can't hide.
   For you I know I'd even try to turn the tide.
   Because you're mine, I walk the line.

I'd Like to Teach the World to Sing

Words and Music by Bill Backer, Roquel Davis, Roger Cook and Roger Greenaway

© 1971, 1972 (Copyrights Renewed) SHADA MUSIC, INC.
All Rights Reserved   Used by Permission

Coda

peace through-out the land. _____ That's the song I hear, ___

Bridge

_____ let the world sing to - day.

Outro

I'd like to teach ___ the world ___ to sing ___ in

per - fect har - mo - ny. _____ Da da da da. _____

Additional Lyrics

2. I'd like to teach the world to sing in perfect harmony.
   I'd like to hold it in my arms and keep it company.

3. I'd like to see the world, for once, all standing hand in hand,
   And hear them echo through the hills for peace throughout the land.

Lean on Me

Words and Music by Bill Withers

Copyright © 1972 INTERIOR MUSIC CORP.
Copyright Renewed
All Rights Controlled and Administered by SONGS OF UNIVERSAL, INC.
All Rights Reserved   Used by Permission

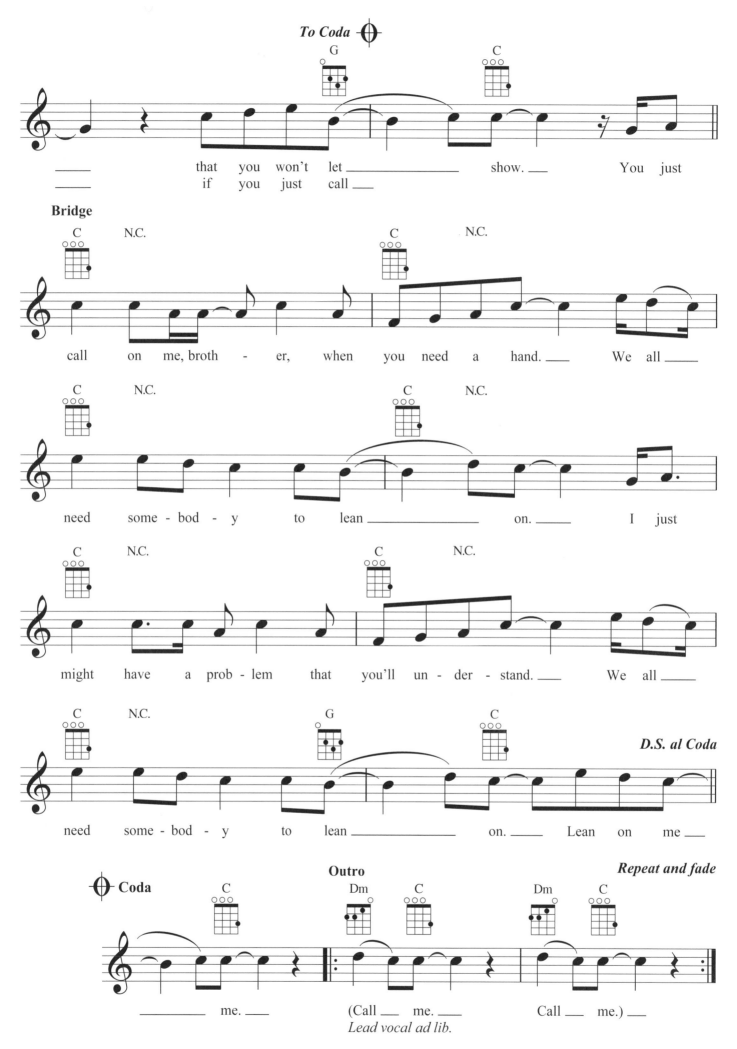

Let It Be

Words and Music by John Lennon and Paul McCartney

Copyright © 1970 Sony/ATV Music Publishing LLC
Copyright Renewed
All Rights Administered by Sony/ATV Music Publishing LLC, 424 Church Street, Suite 1200, Nashville, TN 37219
International Copyright Secured   All Rights Reserved

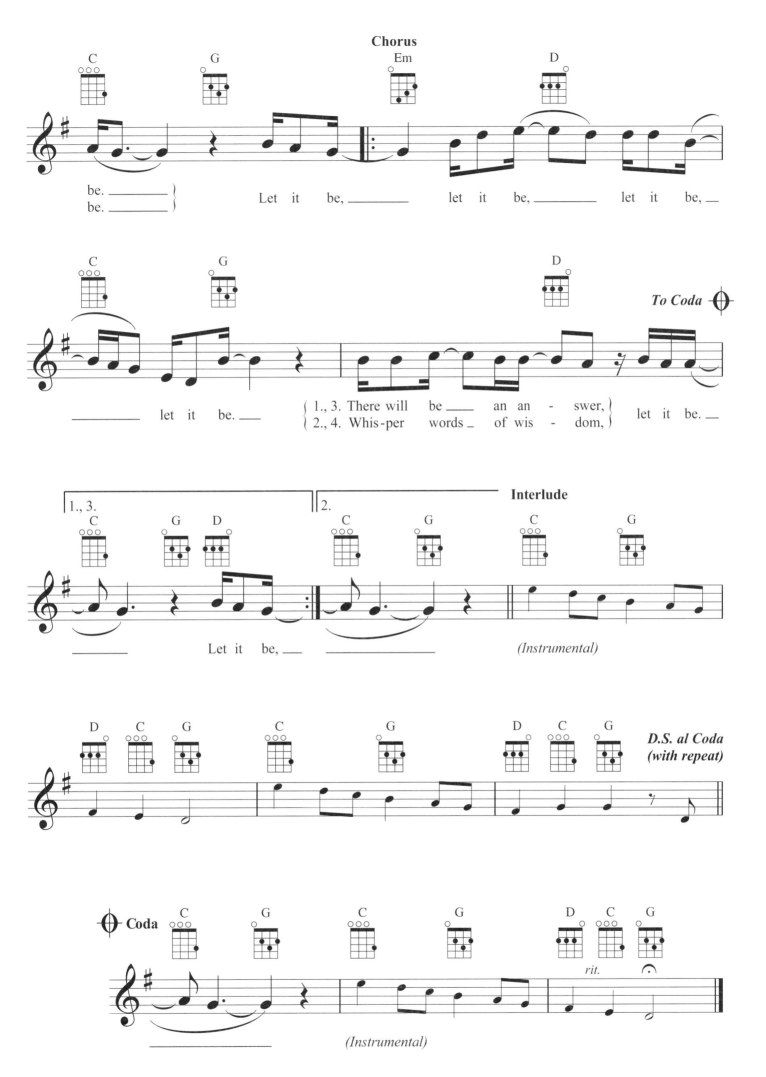

Mountain Dew

Words and Music by Scott Wiseman and Bascomb Lunsford

Copyright © 1945 Sony/ATV Music Publishing LLC and Tannen Music, Inc.
Copyright Renewed
All Rights on behalf of Sony/ATV Music Publishing LLC Administered by Sony/ATV Music Publishing LLC,
424 Church Street, Suite 1200, Nashville, TN 37219
International Copyright Secured   All Rights Reserved

gain with a jug of that good old moun-tain dew.
snort of that good old moun - tain dew.
pint of that good old moun - tain dew.

Chorus

Oh, they call it that old moun - tain

dew, _____ and them that re - fuse it are

few. Oh, I'll hush up my mug if you'll

fill up my jug with that good old moun - tain

1., 2.

3.

dew.

2. Now, the dew. _____

3. Now, ___

On Top of Spaghetti

Words and Music by Tom Glazer

Copyright © 1963 by Songs Music Inc.
Copyright Renewed
All Rights Administered by Larry Spier Music LLC
International Copyright Secured   All Rights Reserved

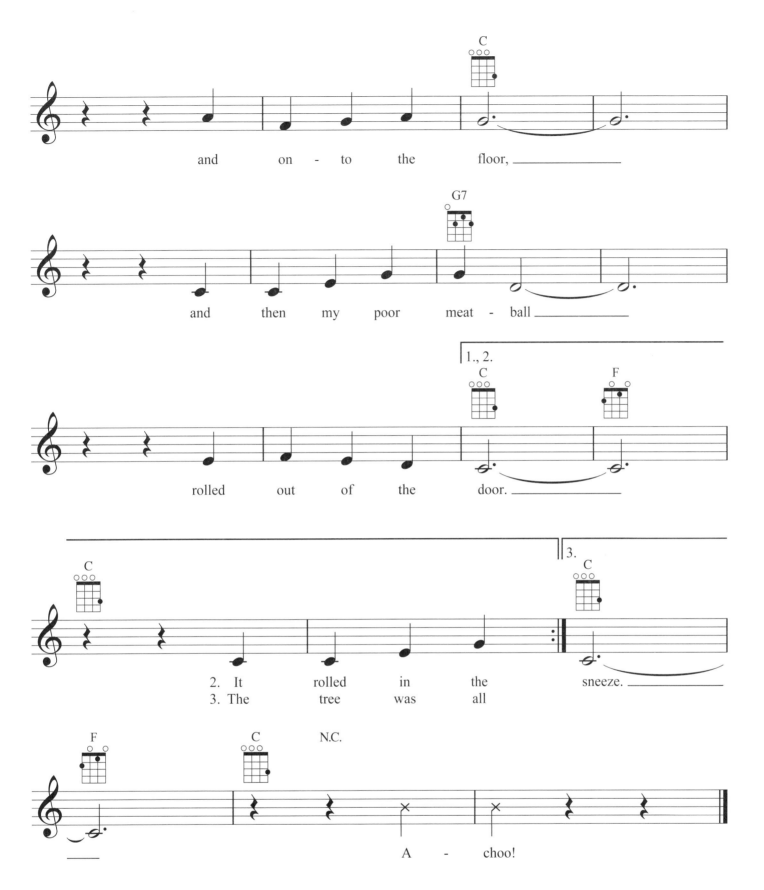

Additional Lyrics

2. It rolled in the garden and under a bush,
   And then my poor meatball was nothing but mush.
   The mush was as tasty as tasty could be,
   And early next summer, it grew into a tree.

3. The tree was all covered with beautiful moss;
   It grew lovely meatballs and tomato sauce.
   So if you eat spaghetti all covered with cheese,
   Hold onto your meatballs and don't ever sneeze.

Peaceful Easy Feeling

Words and Music by Jack Tempchin

© 1972 (Renewed) WB MUSIC CORP. and JAZZ BIRD MUSIC
All Rights Administered by WB MUSIC CORP.
All Rights Reserved   Used by Permission

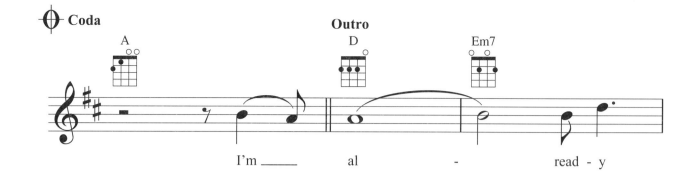

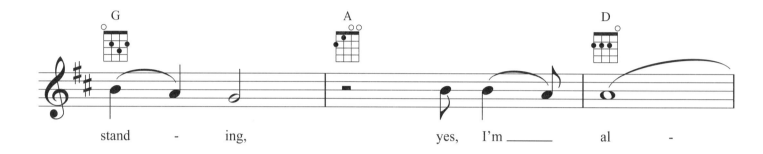

I'm _____ al - read - y

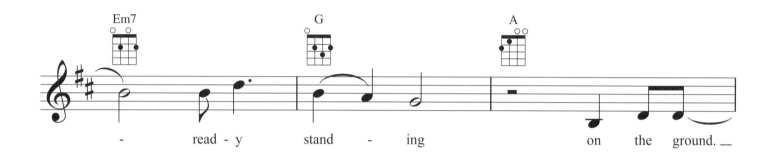

stand - ing,   yes, I'm _____ al -

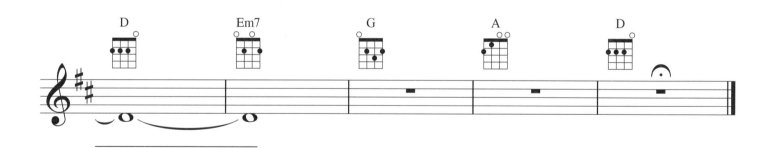

- read - y   stand - ing   on the ground. _

Additional Lyrics

2. And I found out a long time ago
   What a woman can do to your soul.
   Ah, but she can't take you any way
   You don't already know how to go.
   And I got a... *(To Chorus)*

3. I get this feeling I may know you
   As a lover and a friend.
   But this voice keeps whispering in my other ear;
   Tells me I may never see you again.
   'Cause I get a... *(To Chorus)*

The Lion Sleeps Tonight

New Lyrics and Revised Music by George David Weiss, Hugo Peretti and Luigi Creatore

© 1961 FOLKWAYS MUSIC PUBLISHERS, INC.
Copyright Renewed by GEORGE DAVID WEISS, LUIGI CREATORE and JUNE PERETTI
Copyright Assigned to ABILENE MUSIC LLC
All Rights Administered Worldwide by IMAGEM MUSIC LLC
All Rights Reserved   Used by Permission

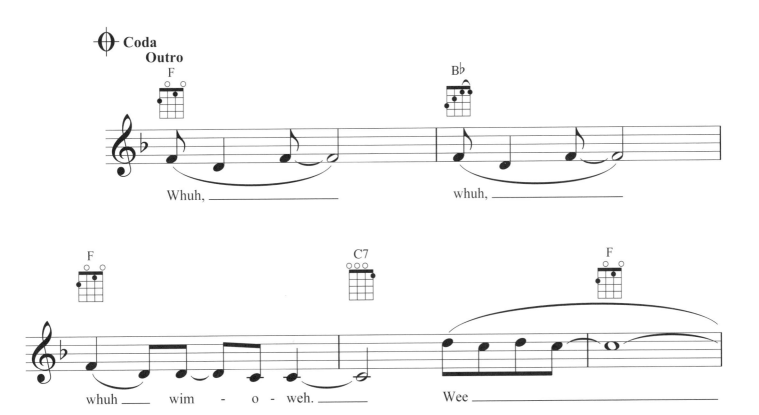

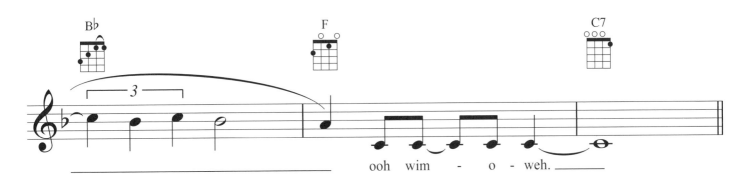

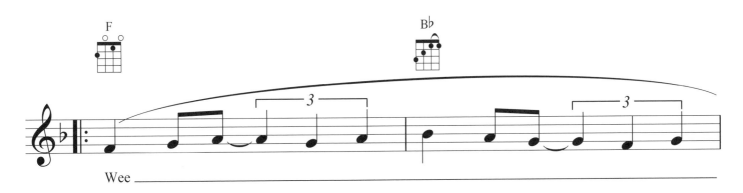

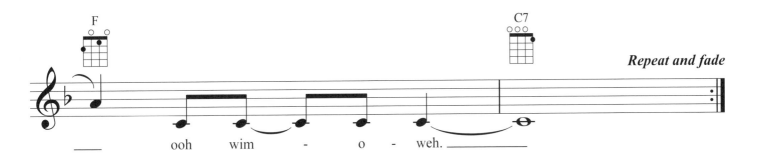

Puff the Magic Dragon

Words and Music by Lenny Lipton and Peter Yarrow

Copyright © 1963; Renewed 1991 Honalee Melodies (ASCAP) and Silver Dawn Music (ASCAP)
Worldwide Rights for Honalee Melodies Administered by BMG Rights Management (US) LLC
Worldwide Rights for Silver Dawn Music Administered by WB Music Corp.
International Copyright Secured   All Rights Reserved

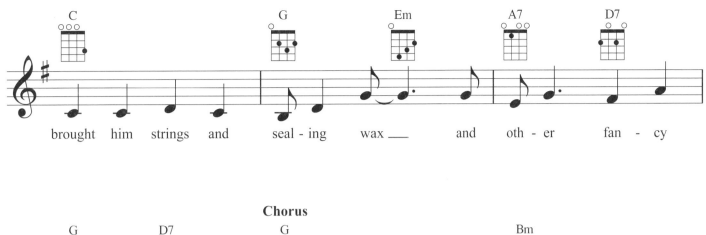

brought him strings and seal - ing wax ___ and oth - er fan - cy

Chorus

stuff. Oh, Puff, the mag - ic drag - on,

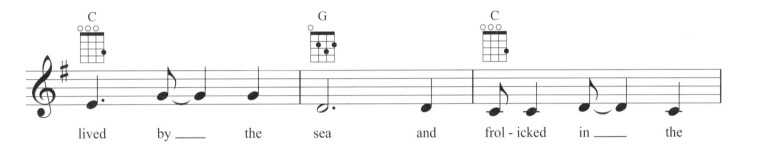

lived by ___ the sea and frol - icked in ___ the

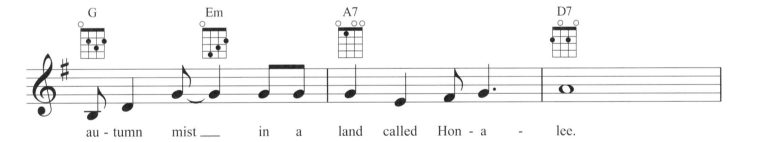

au - tumn mist ___ in a land called Hon - a - lee.

Puff, the mag - ic drag - on, lived by ___ the

sea and frol-icked in _____ the au-tumn mist _____ in a

1., 2.

land called Hon - a - lee.

2. To - land called
3. A

3.

Hon - a - lee. _____

Additional Lyrics

2. Together they would travel on a boat with billowed sail,
   And Jackie kept a lookout perched on Puff's gigantic tail.
   Noble kings and princes would bow whenever they came.
   Pirate ships would lower their flags when Puff roared out his name.

3. A dragon lives forever, but not so little boys.
   Painted wings and giant rings make way for other toys.
   One gray night it happened; Jackie Paper came no more,
   And Puff, that mighty dragon, he ceased his fearless roar. *(To Verse 4)*

4. His head was bent in sorrow, green tears fell like rain.
   Puff no longer went to play along the Cherry Lane.
   Without his lifelong friend, Puff could not be brave.
   So Puff, that mighty dragon, sadly slipped into his cave.

Take Me Home, Country Roads

Words and Music by John Denver, Bill Danoff and Taffy Nivert

Copyright © 1971; Renewed 1999 BMG Ruby Songs, Anna Kate Deutschendorf, Zachary Deutschendorf,
BMG Rights Management (Ireland) Ltd. and Jesse Belle Denver in the U.S.
All Rights for BMG Ruby Songs, Anna Kate Deutschendorf and Zachary Deutschendorf Administered by BMG Rights Management (US) LLC
All Rights for BMG Rights Management (Ireland) Ltd. Administered by Chrysalis One Music
All Rights for Jesse Belle Denver Administered by WB Music Corp.
International Copyright Secured   All Rights Reserved

Sundown

Words and Music by Gordon Lightfoot

First note

Verse
Moderately fast

1. I can see her ly - ing back in her sat - in dress ____ in a
(2.–4.) *See additional lyrics*

room where you do ____ what you don't con - fess. ____ Sun - down, you

bet - ter take care ____ if I find you been creep - in' 'round ____

my back stairs. ____ Sun - down, you

bet - ter take care ____ if I find you been creep - in' 'round ____

© 1973 (Renewed) MOOSE MUSIC LTD.
All Rights Reserved

my back stairs. ___   2. She's been   my back stairs. ___
3., 4. I   can

Outro

Sun - down,   you   bet - ter take care ___ if I
Some - times   I   think it's a   sin ___ when I

find   you been creep - in' 'round ___ my back stairs. ___
feel   like   I'm win - ning when I'm

los - ing a - gain. ___

Additional Lyrics

2. She's been looking like a queen in a sailor's dream,
    And she don't always say what she really means.
    Sometimes I think it's a shame when I get feeling better when I'm feeling no pain.
    Sometimes I think it's a shame when I get feeling better when I'm feeling no pain.

3. I can picture ev'ry move that a man could make.
    Getting lost in her loving is your first mistake.
    Sundown, you better take care if I find you been creepin' 'round my back stairs.
    Sometimes I think it's a sin when I feel like I'm winning when I'm losing again.

4. I can see her looking fast in her faded jeans.
    She's a hard-loving woman, got me feeling mean.
    Sometimes I think it's a shame when I get feeling better when I'm feeling no pain.
    Sundown, you better take care if I find you been creepin' 'round my back stairs.

This Land Is Your Land

Words and Music by Woody Guthrie

WGP/TRO - © Copyright 1956, 1958, 1970, 1972 (Copyrights Renewed) Woody Guthrie Publications, Inc. & Ludlow Music, Inc., New York, NY
administered by Ludlow Music, Inc.
International Copyright Secured
All Rights Reserved Including Public Performance For Profit
Used by Permission

Additional Lyrics

3. When the sun came shining, and I was strolling,
   And the wheat fields waving, and the dust clouds rolling,
   As the fog was lifting, a voice was chanting:
   This land was made for you and me.

4. As I went walking, I saw a sign there,
   And on the sign it said, "No Trespassing,"
   But on the other side it didn't say nothing;
   That side was made for you and me.

5. In the shadow of the steeple, I saw my people.
   By the relief office, I saw my people.
   As they stood there hungry, I stood there asking:
   Is this land made for you and me?

6. Nobody living can ever stop me
   As I go walking that freedom highway.
   Nobody living can ever make me turn back;
   This land was made for you and me.

Tie Me Kangaroo Down Sport

Words and Music by Rolf Harris

© 1960, 1961 (Renewed 1988, 1989) CASTLE MUSIC PTУ. LTD.
All Rights for the U.S. and Canada Controlled and Administered by BEECHWOOD MUSIC CORP.
All Rights Reserved   International Copyright Secured   Used by Permission

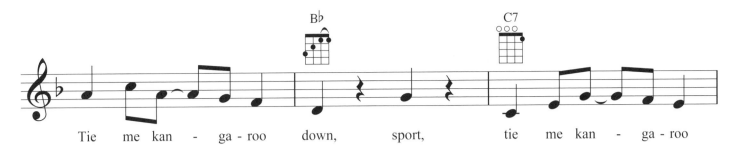

Tie me kan - ga - roo down, sport, tie me kan - ga - roo

down. All to - geth - er now! down.

Additional Lyrics

2. Keep me cockatoo cool, Curl,
   Keep me cockatoo cool.
   Don't go acting the fool, Curl,
   Just keep me cockatoo cool.
   All together now!

3. Take me koala back, Jack,
   Take me koala back.
   He lives somewhere out on the track, Mac,
   So take me koala back.
   All together now!

4. Mind me platypus duck, Bill,
   Mind me platypus duck.
   Don't let him go running amok, Bill,
   Mind me platypus duck.
   All together now!

5. Play your didgeridoo, Blue,
   Play your didgeridoo.
   Keep playing 'til I shoot through, Blue.
   Play your didgeridoo.
   All together now!

6. Tan me hide when I'm dead, Fred,
   Tan me hide when I'm dead.
   So we tanned his hide when he died, Clyde,
   (Spoken:) And that's it hanging on the shed.
   All together now!

The Unicorn

Words and Music by Shel Silverstein

TRO - © Copyright 1962 (Renewed) and 1968 (Renewed) Hollis Music, Inc., New York, NY
International Copyright Secured
All Rights Reserved Including Public Performance For Profit
Used by Permission

Chorus

green al - li - ga - tors and long - necked geese, ___

hump - back cam - els and chim - pan - zees, ___

cats and rats and e - le - phants, but sure as you're born, ___ the

1.–5.

love - li - est of all was the u - ni - corn. 2. But the

6.

u - ni - corn. ___

The Unicorn

(Additional Lyrics)

2. But the Lord seen some sinnin' and it caused him pain.
   He says, "Stand back, I'm gonna make it rain.
   So, hey, Brother Noah, I'll tell you what to do,
   Go and build me a floating zoo."
Chorus: "Two alligators and a couple of geese,
   Two hump-back camels and two chimpanzees,
   Two cats, two rats, two elephants, but sure as you're born,
   Noah, don't you forget my unicorns."

3. Now Noah was there and he answered the callin'
   And he finished up the ark as the rain started fallin'.
   Then he marched in the animals two by two,
   And he sung out as they went through:
Chorus: "Hey, Lord, I got you two alligators and a couple of geese,
   Two hump-back camels and two chimpanzees,
   Two cats, two rats, two elephants, but sure as you're born,
   Lord, I don't see your unicorns."

4. Well, Noah looked out through the drivin' rain,
   But the unicorns was hidin' — playin' silly games.
   They were kickin' and a-spashin' while the rain was pourin',
   Oh, them foolish unicorns.
Chorus: "Hey, Lord, I got you two alligators and a couple of geese,
   Two hump-back camels and two chimpanzees,
   Two cats, two rats, two elephants, but sure as you're born,
   Lord, I don't see your unicorns."

5. Then the ducks started duckin' and the snakes started snakin',
   And the elephants started elephantin' and the boat started shakin',
   The mice started squeakin' and the lions started roarin',
   And everyone's aboard but them unicorns.
Chorus: I mean the two alligators and a couple of geese,
   The hump-back camels and the chimpanzees,
   Noah cried, "Close the door 'cause the rain is pourin',
   And we just can't wait for them unicorns."

6. And then the ark started movin' and it drifted with the tide
   And the unicorns looked up from the rock and cried,
   And the water came up and sort of floated them away.
   That's why you've never seen a unicorn to this day.
Chorus: You'll see a lot of alligators and a whole mess of geese,
   You'll see hump-back camels and chimpanzees,
   You'll see cats and rats and elephants, but sure as you're born,
   You're never gonna see no unicorn.

Wagon Wheel

Words and Music by Ketch Secor and Bob Dylan

First note

Verse
Moderately fast Country

1. Head - in' down south __ to the land of the pines, __ I'm
2., 3. *See additional lyrics*

thumb - in' my way __ out of North __ Car - o - line. __

Starin' up the road __ and pray to God I __ see head -

- lights.

I

made it down the coast in sev - en - teen hours. __ Pick -

Copyright © 2004 BLOOD DONOR MUSIC and SPECIAL RIDER MUSIC
All Rights for BLOOD DONOR MUSIC Controlled and Administered by SPIRIT ONE MUSIC
International Copyright Secured   All Rights Reserved   Used by Permission

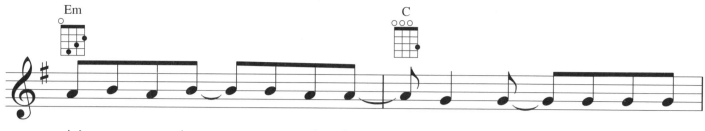

in' me a bou - quet of dog - wood flow'rs. __ And I'm a -

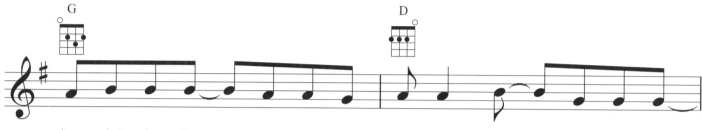

hop - in' for Ra - leigh, I can see my ba - by to - night. __

𝄋 **Chorus**

__ So, rock __ me, ma - ma, like a

wag - on wheel. __ Rock __ me, ma - ma, an - y way you feel. __ Hey, __

__ ma - ma, rock __ me.

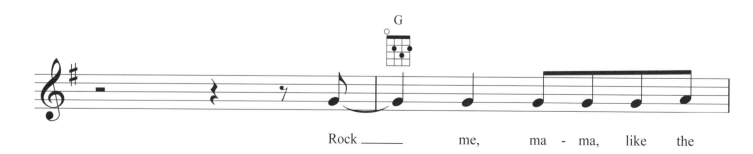

Rock __ me, ma - ma, like the

wind and the rain. ____ Rock ____ me, ma - ma, like a

south - bound train. Hey, _____ ma - ma, rock _

____ me. Oh, _____ so rock _

Oh, _____ so rock _

To Coda ⊕

D.S. al Coda

⊕ **Coda**

Additional Lyrics

2. Runnin' from the cold up in New England,
I was born to be a fiddler in an old-time string band.
My baby plays the guitar, I pick a banjo now.
Oh, North Country winters keep a-gettin' me down.
Lost my money playin' poker, so I had to leave town.
But I ain't turnin' back to livin' that old life no more.

3. Walkin' through the South out of Roanoke,
I caught a trucker out of Philly, had a nice long toke.
But he's a-headin' west from the Cumberland Gap to Johnson City, Tennessee.
I got, I gotta move on before the sun.
I hear my baby callin' my name and I know that she's the only one.
And if I die in Raleigh, at least I will die free.

You Are My Sunshine

Words and Music by Jimmie Davis

Copyright © 1940 by Peer International Corporation
Copyright Renewed
International Copyright Secured   All Rights Reserved

Additional Lyrics

2. I'll always love you and make you happy
   If you will only say the same.
   But if you leave me to love another,
   You'll regret it all someday.

3. You told me once, dear, you really loved me
   And no one else could come between.
   But now you've left me and love another;
   You have shattered all my dreams.

The Best Songs Ever

70 songs have now been arranged for ukulele. Includes: Always • Bohemian Rhapsody • Memory • My Favorite Things • Over the Rainbow • Piano Man • What a Wonderful World • Yesterday • You Raise Me Up • and more.

00282413 . . . . $17.99

Campfire Songs for Ukulele

30 favorites to sing as you roast marshmallows and strum your uke around the campfire. Includes: God Bless the U.S.A. • Hallelujah • The House of the Rising Sun • I Walk the Line • Puff the Magic Dragon • Wagon Wheel • You Are My Sunshine • and more.

00129170 . . . . $14.99

The Daily Ukulele

arr. Liz and Jim Beloff
Strum a different song everyday with easy arrangements of 365 of your favorite songs in one big songbook! Includes favorites by the Beatles, Beach Boys, and Bob Dylan, folk songs, pop songs, kids' songs, Christmas carols, and Broadway and Hollywood tunes, all with a spiral binding for ease of use.

00240356 Original Edition. $39.99
00240681 Leap Year Edition $39.99
00119270 Portable Edition $37.50

Disney Hits for Ukulele

Play 23 of your favorite Disney songs on your ukulele. Includes: The Bare Necessities • Cruella De Vil • Do You Want to Build a Snowman? • Kiss the Girl • Lava • Let It Go • Once upon a Dream • A Whole New World • and more.

00151250 . . . . $16.99

Also available:
00291547 **Disney Fun Songs for Ukulele** . . . $16.99
00701708 **Disney Songs for Ukulele** $14.99
00334696 **First 50 Disney Songs on Ukulele** . $16.99

First 50 Songs You Should Play on Ukulele

An amazing collec-tion of 50 accessible, must-know favorites: Edelweiss • Hey, Soul Sister • I Walk the Line • I'm Yours • Imagine • Over the Rainbow • Peaceful Easy Feeling • The Rainbow Connection • Riptide • more.

00149250 . . . . $16.99

Also available:
00292082 **First 50 Melodies on Ukulele** . . . $15.99
00289029 **First 50 Songs on Solo Ukulele** . . $15.99
00347437 **First 50 Songs to Strum on Uke** . $16.99

40 Most Streamed Songs for Ukulele

40 top hits that sound great on uke! Includes: Despacito • Feel It Still • Girls like You • Happier • Havana • High Hopes • The Middle • Perfect • 7 Rings • Shallow • Shape of You • Something Just like This • Stay • Sucker • Sunflower • Sweet but Psycho • Thank U, Next • There's Nothing Holdin' Me Back • Without Me • and more!

00298113 . . . . $17.99

The 4 Chord Songbook

With just 4 chords, you can play 50 hot songs on your ukulele! Songs include: Brown Eyed Girl • Do Wah Diddy Diddy • Hey Ya! • Ho Hey • Jessie's Girl • Let It Be • One Love • Stand by Me • Toes • With or Without You • and many more.

00142050 . . . . $16.99

Also available:
00141143 **The 3-Chord Songbook** $16.99

Pop Songs for Kids

30 easy pop favorites for kids to play on uke, including: Brave • Can't Stop the Feeling! • Feel It Still • Fight Song • Happy • Havana • House of Gold • How Far I'll Go • Let It Go • Remember Me (Ernesto de la Cruz) • Rewrite the Stars • Roar • Shake It Off • Story of My Life • What Makes You Beautiful • and more.

00284415 . . . . $16.99

Simple Songs for Ukulele

50 favorites for standard G-C-E-A ukulele tuning, including: All Along the Watchtower • Can't Help Falling in Love • Don't Worry, Be Happy • Hey Hey • I'm Yours • King of the Road • Sweet Home Alabama • You Are My Sunshine • and more.

00156815 . . . . $14.99

Also available:
00276644 **More Simple Songs for Ukulele** . $14.99

Top Hits of 2020

18 uke-friendly tunes of 2020 are featured in this collection of melody, lyric and chord arrangements in standard G-C-E-A tuning. Includes: Adore You (Harry Styles) • Before You Go (Lewis Capaldi) • Cardigan (Taylor Swift) • Daisies (Katy Perry) • I Dare You (Kelly Clarkson) • Level of Concern (twenty one pilots) • No Time to Die (Billie Eilish) • Rain on Me (Lady Gaga feat. Ariana Grande) • Say So (Doja Cat) • and more.

00355553 . . . . $14.99

Also available:
00302274 **Top Hits of 2019** $14.99

Ukulele: The Most Requested Songs

Strum & Sing Series
Cherry Lane Music
Nearly 50 favorites all expertly arranged for ukulele! Includes: Bubbly • Build Me Up Buttercup • Cecilia • Georgia on My Mind • Kokomo • L-O-V-E • Your Body Is a Wonderland • and more.

02501453 . . . . $14.99

The Ultimate Ukulele Fake Book

Uke enthusiasts will love this giant, spiral-bound collection of over 400 songs for uke! Includes: Crazy • Dancing Queen • Downtown • Fields of Gold • Happy • Hey Jude • 7 Years • Summertime • Thinking Out Loud • Thriller • Wagon Wheel • and more.

00175500 9" x 12" Edition $45.00
00319997 5.5" x 8.5" Edition $39.99

HAL•LEONARD®

Order today from your favorite music retailer at
halleonard.com

Prices, contents and availability subject to change without notice

Disney characters and artwork TM & © 2021 Disney

0621
479